Developing Emotional Intelligence

Angus Robertson

Copyright © 2021 by Angus Robertson

All rights reserved.

No portion of this book may be reproduced in any form without written permission from the publisher or author, except as permitted by U.S. copyright law.

Contents

1. Introduction   1
2. What is Emotional Intelligence   3
3. Categories of Emotional Intelligence   4
4. Social Skills   6
5. Benefits of High Emotional Intelligence   7
6. How to identify emotional triggers and strategies for dealing with them   10
7. How to deal with emotional triggers   12
8. Why you need to take responsibility and set personal boundaries   14
9. How to Increase Your Emotional Intelligence   17
10. The Essential Keys to Commanding Your Emotions   19
11. How to manage anger and gain emotional control   22
12. Emotional intelligence is a powerful tool for conflict resolution   25
13. Mastering Your Interpersonal Skills for Higher Emotional Intelligence   27
14. Conclusion   29

Chapter One

Introduction

The idea of emotional intelligence (or EQ) has gained popularity over the past decade. Unfortunately, many people don't understand the meaning of EQ or why it became so popular in the past few years. Numerous scientific studies over the years have shown that emotional intelligence is far more important than average intelligence, which is measured using the IQ scale.

These studies were conducted by universities in America and Europe. They found that only 20% of our successes and achievements can be attributed to the common intelligence response. The other 80 per cent relies solely on our emotional intelligence.

Everybody, from CEOs to students, is constantly confronted with their emotions and those of others. Your ability to manage your emotions can have a profound impact on how others perceive you and how effective you are at getting things done. You can improve your emotional intelligence and be able to handle stressful situations with maturity. John Mayer and Peter Salovey and Konstantin Vasily Peterides, renowned researchers, discovered that people with high emotional intelligence are more effective leaders and achieve greater success in all they do.

Wayne Payne, in his doctoral thesis A Study of Emotion: Building Emotional Intelligence, was the first to use the term "emotional intelligence". He compared IQ and emotional intelligence in his thesis and concluded that EQ is superior as it encompasses a broad range of faculties and aspects. Understanding your emotional intelligence can help you understand your emotions and their impact. This is essential because it improves one's self-awareness. You will be able to better understand the behavior and underlying causes of others by studying your EQ.

People who are emotionally intelligent can reconcile their reason and mind with their emotions and feel the truth of their feelings. This skill makes emotionally intelligent people self-confident, self-aware and creative. They also have a lot of other skills.

They are more capable of managing stress and can learn to get along with others. They approach life with optimism and are less afraid of change. They are the people who succeed.

Chapter Two

What is Emotional Intelligence

Emotional intelligence (or EQ) refers to the ability to recognize, understand, use and manage emotions in a positive way. It can be used to improve communication, overcome challenges and alleviate stress. Emotional intelligence covers many aspects of our everyday lives, including how we act and interact with others.

Emotionally intelligent people are more able to identify their own emotions and those of others. Understanding the emotions of others around you will help you better connect with them, have healthier relationships and live a happier life.

Emotional intelligence is more important than intelligence quotient (IQ) in achieving success in your career and in your personal life. How far you go in your professional and personal pursuits will depend on how well you can read and interpret the signals of others and respond appropriately to them. It is important to have a high level of emotional intelligence. This will enable you to understand, negotiate, and empathize.

Chapter Three

Categories of Emotional Intelligence

Research in the field of emotional intelligence found that there are five main classes of skills that can be associated with emotional intelligence.

Self-Awareness

Self-awareness refers to your ability to recognize your emotions and their impact on your thoughts and behaviour. Self-awareness is essential for emotional intelligence. It will help you to recognize your strengths and weaknesses. Self-awareness can also improve your self-confidence.

Self-Regulation

Self-regulation refers to your ability to put impulse behaviours and feelings under control. It is another important part of emotional intelligence. Self-management does not prevent you from feeling emotions. However, it allows you to control how long they last. Self-regulation is about learning how to manage emotions healthily, adapt to changing situations, and follow through on your commitments.

You can use a variety of techniques to reduce negative emotions such as anger and depression. Meditation and recasting situations positively are two of the options. These are the attributes of self-regulation:

* Self-control
* Trustworthiness
* Conscientiousness
* Adaptability
* Innovation

Motivation

Motivation is the inner process that drives you towards a goal. This type of emotional intelligence requires that you set clear goals and have a path to reach them.

positive attitude. Everybody has a predisposition to a positive or negative outlook. However, with some motivation, you can change your thinking and shift your focus to a more positive one. You can change every negative thought you have in your head to make it positive and help you reach your goals. These are the key ingredients of motivation:

* Achievement drive
* Commitment
* Initiative
* Optimism

Empathy

Empathy is the ability to empathize with others' emotions, concerns, and needs. It is an essential component of emotional intelligence. Empathy allows you to identify emotional cues, group power dynamics and help you respond more effectively to others' reactions. Empathetic people excel in developing others, serving others, leveraging diversity and political awareness.

Chapter Four

Social Skills

Social skills are the final category of emotional intelligence. The ability to build interpersonal skills, also known as relationship management, can greatly increase your chances of a successful career. It is vital to have interpersonal skills in order to communicate effectively with people. You will be able to manage conflict and have great social skills.

* Influence others
* Communicate
* Lead

Psychologists agree that IQ alone doesn't guarantee happiness or success. Recent studies show that your IQ is only 10-25 percent of your success. Emotional intelligence is about 75 percent. Studies have shown that people with higher EQ scores perform better at work and are more confident and better leaders. These factors all point to the importance of EQ and how it can greatly improve a person's productivity and personal growth.

Chapter Five

Benefits of High Emotional Intelligence

A high level of emotional intelligence will help you stand out from the crowd and open up new opportunities. High emotional intelligence can bring many benefits to your life. The good news is that anyone who is willing and able to improve their emotional intelligence levels can do so if they are willing to put in the effort.

There are many people in the world who are extremely smart but don't have the life they want. There are many people who excel in academics but are not great in personal relationships. This is because they are not able to communicate with their families.

Despite having a high IQ and a low emotional intelligence, they may still be very intelligent. Emotional intelligence can help you achieve many things, including the following.

Personal effectiveness

Your success is dependent on your emotional intelligence. You will be able to successfully manage your own affairs and the affairs of others. You can increase your personal effectiveness by using emotional intelligence strategies and tools that make you more aware of your emotions.

Thinking Skills

It may not be the complexity of an issue that makes it difficult to solve, but your perspective. You can solve old problems by changing your perspective. Emotional intelligence is also helpful in developing your strategic thinking ability and your ability inspire and motivate your team.

Professional Relationships

You will have a greater emotional intelligence and be better able to understand what makes people tick. This is essential in creating a positive work environment and building relationships.

Your ability to communicate effectively and interact with others can be improved by increasing your emotional intelligence. This will result in a better professional relationship.

Leadership Capability

Leadership requires empathy and understanding of the people you lead. You can use emotional intelligence to persuade, influence, motivate, and inspire others. Success in leadership or management is determined by how well you can understand and respond to others' emotions. This will increase satisfaction and foster stronger workplace relationships.

Physical well-being

Your overall well-being is directly affected by your emotional intelligence. Your emotional intelligence is directly related to stress management. This gives you the ability to respond positively to any challenges you face in your life. This is vital because stress can lead to a decrease in your physical abilities, lower your immune system, and ultimately, a reduction in your quality of your life.

Mental Well-Being

Emotional intelligence can influence your outlook and attitude about life. Low EQ can lead to depression, anxiety, mood swings, and other mental disorders. You will experience a decline in your optimism and positivity, which can make your life less enjoyable and dull. Mental stability is best when all of your faculties are functioning properly, including your ability understand and interpret emotions.

Conflict Management

Conflict is something you can't avoid. Your ability to resolve disputes is dependent on your ability understand the emotions of those involved. It is easier to resolve conflicts if you are able to empathize and understand the emotions of those involved. Because you can see the needs and desires of the disputing parties, high emotional intelligence makes you a better negotiator. It is easier to resolve conflict when you understand the bones of contention.

Success

Your internal motivations and self-confidence are key factors in your ability to stay focused on a goal. Higher levels of emotional intelligence may help you to be more self-reliant and stay on track towards your goals. Emotional intelligence can help you build a stronger support network, overcome obstacles with incredible resilience, and overcome any setbacks.

Your success is your success. A person who is emotionally intelligent can put off immediate gratification to focus on the long-term results of a course that will increase your chances of success.

Although the field of emotional intelligence continues to attract research from different scholars, it is clear that emotions play an important role in improving our personal and professional lives. While technology has allowed us to access more information, it has not made it possible to manage our emotions.

Chapter Six

How to identify emotional triggers and strategies for dealing with them

Emotional triggers can be thoughts, feelings, or events that can trigger an immediate response. Because the reaction happens automatically and without any control, it is important to use the term trigger. These reactions may seem uncontrollable, but in reality, as with everything else, we have the power to choose how we respond. You can learn to identify your emotional triggers to help you take control of how you react to different situations.

How to identify your emotional triggers

You will never be able to recognize your emotional triggers. They will continue to rule your emotions. Instead of letting minor problems make you feel like you are running for your life, learn how to manage your emotions. This can be done by first addressing your own stressors. There are many stressors that can be identified, such as the ones listed below.

Stressors for the Emotions

Internal stressors may also include emotional stressors. These stressors include anxiety, fears, personality traits such as perfectionism, suspiciousness, pessimism and pessimism. These stressors can cause you to have distorted thinking and perceptions about others.

Family Stressors

These stressors include financial problems, relationship problems and empty nest syndrome. These issues can all trigger an emotional response.

Social Stressors

The interactions you have with others can cause social stressors. These stressors can also include public speaking.

Parties, dating, and other social events. Social stressors, just like emotional stressors and parties, are individual.

Change Stressors

These stressors can be caused by life changes. These stressors include moving to a different location, starting a job, marriage, or having children.

Work Stressors

Stressors at work are those that happen in an environment where there is often a lot of pressure. These stressors include a boss who is unpredictable, unfinished tasks, and tight deadlines.

These stressors are not the only ones that can impact your emotional intelligence. These include the following: decision, disease and phobic, pain, environmental, and others. Using the list of stressors, you will be able to identify the most significant stressors in your daily life. You might find that your stressors are not all in one category.

Chapter Seven

How to deal with emotional triggers

Once you have identified the stressors in you life, it is time to determine how you can deal with them individually. These are some common strategies people use to manage emotional triggers.

Elimination

You can eliminate some of the emotional triggers in your life. If you don't feel at ease in a community, you might be able to relocate to another area to start a new life. You will be able to eliminate all social stressors from your life. You have two options for your workplace: you can ask for a transfer, or find another job. Some stressors are difficult to eliminate. If you don't want to lose your job, it could be very costly. These stressors can be dealt with using other strategies.

Reduce Stressors' Strength

This strategy is great because it allows you to live with others and minimizes the stressors. You might consider purchasing a pair of earplugs if you find that the noise from your neighbour distracts you from focusing on your task. You might feel stressed about your commute to work because you drive more than two hours.

You might consider using public transport or carpooling with colleagues from work.

Coping

You can't beat them so join them. You may have to learn to live with most stressors. It could prove counterproductive to eliminate them from your life. It is important to find coping strategies that allow you to remain calm and clear-headed even under pressure. These techniques will make it less stressful to you.

Talking to a friend

Talking to a friend who is trustworthy can help you deal with stressors. You can receive support, encouragement, and new ideas by talking to a trusted friend. Because the feedback you get is from an outside perspective, it's important to take into consideration what you are hearing. You can join a support group if you are unable to find someone to talk to. These support groups have life coaches with experience dealing with emotional triggers.

Keep Positive

Our perspective can make a difference in how emotional triggers are perceived. It is unlikely that emotional triggers can take a toll on your outlook if you stay positive. There are situations in life that can trigger emotions. However, if you keep your eyes on the positive, these situations may not turn your world upside-down.

You can live a happy life by avoiding anxiety. Instead of dwelling on the problems of the past or worrying about the uncertain future, focus on the present and take advantage of any opportunities.

Each person is different, but each one is sensitive to emotions to a degree. Learning how to manage these emotions and triggers is what makes us unique.

Chapter Eight

Why you need to take responsibility and set personal boundaries

Whatever happened in your life, you are ultimately responsible for it. This principle is essential if you want to find happiness and success in both your professional and personal lives. You can always blame others when things go wrong, but this won't help your quest for happiness.

It will only make the situation worse and lead to more irresponsibility. The most effective and intelligent way to deal with life's problems is to take responsibility for your choices, actions, and direction. You will see your life differently if you don't take responsibility. And you will find yourself blaming others for your problems more often.

You can take full responsibility for your life and feel joy and control despite all the circumstances. This will allow you to make better choices and decisions because you fully understand that only you and you alone are responsible for what happens. You have control over how you react to events that are outside your control. Either you make the situation worse or you can use it to help you climb higher.

How to take responsibility

You must accept that you are responsible for your own life and that no one can take it away from you. No matter how much you try to convince others that the current events in your life are not the result of your actions, it is essential that you go through them and deal with the consequences. These are the steps you need to take to stay in control and manage the situations that you face with determination and resolve.

Don't Blame Others

You need to be able to hear yourself, whether you're speaking alone or with others. Be free from excuses and blame in your speech. You will continue to blame others.

The more you speak in your mind, then the more likely it is that you will attempt to shift responsibility to other people.

Take feedback seriously

Sometimes you may not be able hear the words you are speaking with others. Accepting feedback from others is crucial to your emotional intelligence. You might find that some people are observant enough to share their thoughts with you about how you shift blame to others. This kind of feedback can make a big difference in your life and how you see it. We are prone to reject feedback that isn't in our favor. You will be more likely to continue your reckless tendencies to your detriment if you reject the observations of others.

Plan Your Life

Your life is the sum of all your decisions and actions on a daily basis. You can take control of your life and stop blaming others. You should break down your plan into manageable goals that you can track your progress.

Recognizing Your Choices

The overall decision about how you will respond to any situation is yours. It doesn't matter how severe the situation is. You can be kept in prison without losing your mental health. It is possible to look at a positive outcome than the current situation. This will allow you to release your emotions, and more importantly, your whole being.

How to set your personal boundaries

It is important to learn how to establish boundaries once you have a better understanding of your personal boundaries and what makes them healthy. It will take time to set personal boundaries. You need patience.

Take a look at your boundaries

If you don't know what personal boundaries are, it is nearly impossible to set and enforce them. Consider the things that are making you feel uncomfortable. Consider the possibilities of other people entering your life. Also consider the appropriate actions they should take. This will allow you to draw clear lines and help you define your personal boundaries.

Describe Your Needs

Do not be afraid to tell those around you what you need. If you are annoyed by someone's noise, it is important to be able to tell them you want silence. This will signal to them that they are intruding into your privacy.

Keep the Consequences in Your Hands

As with any boundary violation (physical or emotional), there must be consequences. Individuals may be open to experimentation and make minor violations to see if there are consequences. If there are no consequences, they will continue to infringe on your personal boundaries. They might even try to create a new code for how they deal with you. To stop others from crossing your personal boundaries, you must set up consequences.

Stand firm

You must hold firm to your values and ideals if you want to establish and maintain personal boundaries. You are in the moment

If you make a mistake or compromise your position, others will also be affected.

It is easy to get in on the action and break your boundaries.

How you define and take responsibility for your space is an indicator of emotional intelligence. An emotionally intelligent person is one who has a clear value system and clearly identifies boundaries.

Chapter Nine

How to Increase Your Emotional Intelligence

Your senses must first receive the information before it can enter your brain. Your natural instincts will take control of this information, making it difficult for us to act when it is emotionally charged or overwhelming. You need to be able to manage your emotions and make sound decisions in these situations.

Your memory is strongly linked to emotion. You will have more options when you respond to new situations if you can connect to your emotional and rational brain. You can also avoid repeating past errors by incorporating emotional memory into your decision-making process.

The Key Skills of Emotional Intelligence

You can improve your emotional intelligence, your decision-making ability and your ability to make good decisions by learning how to deal with your emotions in every situation. You will need to learn how to manage and control your stress levels in order to do this. Anyone can learn these skills if they are willing to put the knowledge into practice.

You can change your behavior to resist pressure permanently by learning how to overcome stress and maintain emotional awareness.

Rapid Stress Reduction

Although stress is an inevitable part of daily life, it can also cause problems in the body and mind. Stress can also make it difficult to communicate clearly and interfere with our ability read situations accurately.

You need to be able to stay focused, balanced, in control and to maintain your focus, no matter how stressful it is. You can use stress-busting to manage stressful situations. These steps will help you develop stress-busting skills.

Take note of your physical response

You need to understand how your body reacts to stress to be able to manage your emotions and decrease the negative effects of stress on your life. You can learn how you feel when you're under stress to help regulate tension.

Stress can cause different reactions in people. Some people may become angry or agitated if they are faced with stressful situations, while others might withdraw and feel depressed. Stress-relieving events will be a good choice for you if you tend to get angry. If you are prone to becoming depressed due to stress, it is best to find activities that stimulate you.

Examine the Stress-Busting Techniques That Work for You

Engaging your senses is one of the fastest ways to reduce stress. Each person responds to these sensory inputs differently. The trick is finding things that soothe you or that give you energy. If you're a visual person, surround yourself with positive images to reduce stress. If you prefer sound, you might find music that helps you relax.

Emotional Awareness

Understanding yourself requires the ability to connect with your emotions. Emotional awareness can help you become calm and focused even in stressful situations. Many people today feel disconnected from their emotions due to negative childhood experiences that taught them how to suppress their feelings when confronted with stressful situations.

We can only deny, alter, or numb our emotions, but we cannot eliminate them. No matter how we deal with our emotions, they are still there. If you're emotionally uninformed, you can't fully understand your emotions, which will make you more vulnerable to becoming overwhelmed in dangerous situations. To achieve emotional intelligence, it is important to connect with your emotions again and to learn to accept them.

Your emotional awareness can be developed at any moment. As with all developmental processes, improving your emotional awareness should be gradual. Start with stress management and then move on to learning how you can reconnect with your stronger emotions. This will allow you to change how you feel and how you respond to them.

Chapter Ten

The Essential Keys to Commanding Your Emotions

You can master your emotions and ultimately control your life. Understanding why you do what you do is crucial. If you want to earn more money, lose weight or purchase new clothes, this is because you feel fulfilled when you achieve your goals. People who believe losing weight will make them more confident and attract the right person into their lives will do anything to lose it.

Emotions are an important part of life. Instead of ignoring them or hiding them, acknowledge them and discover the truth within.

The Emotional Triad

Whatever situation you find yourself in, there three factors that will influence your feelings about it. These factors are known as the Emotional Triad by psychologists. They include:

Your Physiology

Your body is the first place you feel every emotion in your life. If you want to feel more confident in your speech, you must be grounded, strong, and principled. If you want to feel more passion and joy in your life, you need to talk more often.

If you want to feel sad, all you have to do is frown, take a deep breath, look at the ground, and then stare down. It is important to realize that your body's actions can have an impact on how you feel. Motion is what creates emotion.

What should you be focusing on?

How you use your body will determine how you feel. However, it is not only how you use it that matters. What you focus on can also affect how you feel. You can feel happy if you focus your attention on the things that make you happy. You can make a positive impact on your life by recollecting the more joyous moments from your past. You can eliminate all positive experiences and good things in your life and instead focus on the negative.

You will feel depressed. There are both good and bad things in life. It is up to you what you choose to focus on.

Your Language

Your words can have a profound effect on how you feel. You will likely feel tired and bored if you start making statements such as "I'm exhausted" or "I am so bored". Every word you use has an emotional meaning. Some words you use can be disempowering while others can be encouraging and uplifting. You can manage your emotions by being mindful of your vocabulary, phrases, metaphors, sentences, and phrases.

The Emotional Triad teaches us that happiness can be a choice. This is true for anger, depression, frustration, and all three. It is not possible to make someone happy or angry. Instead, it all depends on how you interpret each situation in your life.

How to deal with negative emotions

Negative and positive emotions are part of everyday life and cannot be ignored. You can choose to address these emotions in order to effectively suppress them.

Positive emotions can be encouraged and replaced by negative ones. There are four methods to deal with negative emotions.

Avoidance

Avoidance is simply avoiding situations that could trigger negative emotions. You might avoid interacting with strangers or take risks because of fear of rejection or failure. People often resort to self-medication such as alcohol or drugs to avoid negative emotions.

Denialism

You can denial be the act of denying the negative emotions that you feel by saying things like "It wasn't that bad." Unfortunately, this approach will only increase the negative emotions and make it more difficult to pay attention to them.

Learn and use your negative emotions

One way to overcome negative emotions is to learn from them and use them to your advantage. You must first realize that all emotions, positive and negative, are there for you. Your daily emotions can be a guideline, support system or call to action. These emotions will tell you if the activity you're participating in works or not.

Remember that your emotions are created by you, and only you can control them. It doesn't matter if you have a reason to feel this way. You can choose your own reasons. You have the power to control your emotions.

You are the only one who can handle them all. You are the only person who can manage every emotion. You can learn to take advantage of your emotions, and make them work for you instead of against you.

Chapter Eleven

How to manage anger and gain emotional control

Anger can cause you to engage in fights or arguments with others. Anger can be a healthy emotion. However, if it becomes chronic, it can spiral out of control. Uncontrolled anger can have severe consequences for your life, your mental health, your emotional intelligence, and your physical well-being.

You can learn how to manage your anger by understanding the causes of your anger.

Understanding Anger

Anger is a emotion that can be either good or bad. Anger is a natural emotion that you can display when you are wronged or mistreated. Although anger is not a problem, it can make a huge difference in how you handle your anger. Anger can cause harm to you and others.

Many people believe that anger control is difficult when one has a fiery temper. We have much more control than we realize over our anger. It is possible to learn how to communicate your emotions without hurting others. This will make you feel better and help you meet your needs faster. Although anger management can be difficult to master, it is possible to improve your skills. Your ability to manage anger can have a significant impact on your ability to achieve your goals, your relationships and your overall satisfaction with your life.

The importance of anger management

Many people believe they are entitled to their anger and others around them have too much empathy. Anger can be very damaging to your relationships and can impair your judgement. Emotional outbursts are a hindrance to success and can have a negative effect on the performance of others.

You are what you see. Anger can spiral out of control and even cause damage to your physical health.

High levels of stress and tension can be detrimental to your health. Research has shown that chronic anger can increase your risk of heart disease, high cholesterol, diabetes and a weak immune system.

Anger can cause you to consume a lot of mental energy. This can lead to a lot of thoughts and feelings. This can lead to a decrease in your ability to focus, see the bigger picture, and have a good time. People who experience frequent anger are more likely to suffer from depression and stress.

Anger management can have a negative impact on your career success. While constructive criticism and creative differences are good for your career, stoking anger can cause you to lose respect and lead to a poor reputation.

Anger can also cause harm to relationships.

Friendships are important. People will not trust you if you are always angry.

Tips for Managing Your Anger

You need to understand why anger management is important and how you can avoid it spiraling out of control.

These are some practical and useful tips that will help you control your anger.

Understanding the Root Cause of your Anger

There is no reason for anything to happen. An underlying problem must be causing your anger. Many of your anger stems from childhood experiences. If you were raised in a violent home, anger might be a way to express your frustrations and get what you want. Anger can also be caused by stress or trauma.

Anger can be used by some people to hide their feelings of vulnerability, insecurity, shame, shame, or hurt. These people don't really feel angry but instead connect to certain emotions.

Events that anger them. Evidence of knee-jerk reactions is evidence

The temper being displayed is just a cover-up of other emotions and needs.

Be aware of warning signs and anger triggers

Warning signs are present for every anger explosion. These signs can be physical and manifest through your body. Anger is a fuel for the fight or flight system within your body. The more angry you are, the greater the chances that your body will go into overdrive. You can manage your temper by taking the time to learn about your body's warning signs.

It's easy to blame others for everything. But, it is much easier to focus on the person or thing that is causing your anger and not how you react to stressful situations. It has little to do the actions of others.

Find Cooling Methods That Work

There are many techniques you can use in order to calm down and control your anger. These are some of the techniques:

* Take deep, slow breaths from your abdomen and take deep inhalations.

Exercise can help to release energy and make it easier to approach situations with a cool head.

Use all of your senses to calm down.

Massages and stretching areas that are tight can be a great way to help you.

Relax your body and let go of tension.

To help you let go of tension and allow you to have the space to rethink your responses, you can remove yourself from the situation.

Get professional help

Professional help is recommended if you are unable to manage your anger by yourself. There are programs, classes, and therapies that are designed for anger management issues. You can share your problems with others, and you can work together to overcome them.

Chapter Twelve

Emotional intelligence is a powerful tool for conflict resolution

Each relationship is unique and has its ups as well as downs. Conflict is an integral part of any relationship. Emotional intelligence is about learning how to manage conflict, rather than trying to resolve it.

If conflict is not managed well, there are good chances that it will lead to significant damage to your relationships. You can strengthen your relationships by learning how to manage conflict constructively and respectfully. It is essential to learn how to resolve disputes in order for you and your relationships to improve.

Understanding the Cause of Conflict

Both small and large differences can lead to conflict. Conflict is inevitable when people have different motivations, ideas and values. While small differences can fuel conflict, the core of conflict is often a deeper-seated personal need. These needs could be anything, from safety to respect, and everything in-between.

How to perceive conflict

Different people perceive conflict in different ways. Because of their painful pasts, some people will try to avoid conflict. You might think that conflict is only possible if you have had bad relationships in the past. Conflict in relationships is often seen as demoralizing, humiliating and dangerous. It should also be something to be afraid of. Conflict can be traumatizing if you have had a difficult childhood.

Your prophecy will likely be fulfilled if you see conflict as dangerous. It can be more difficult to manage conflict well if you are feeling threatened when you get into conflict. You will likely either explode in anger or shut down completely.

Conflict Resolution Skills

Two core skills are essential to successfully resolve conflict. This is the ability reduce stress quickly and the second is the ability remove emotions from your body so you can respond constructively to attacks or arguments.

Quick Stress Relief

You can improve your stress management skills to help you stay focused and balanced no matter what the circumstances. If you lose your ability to remain centered and in control, you are more likely to become overwhelmed by conflict situations, which can affect the quality of how you respond. Stress can cause tension and tightness in the body.

Emotional Awareness

Empathy helps you to understand yourself and others. You won't be able resolve conflicts in your life if you don't feel the same way. Effective communication is key to conflict resolution.

Although it may seem easy to understand your emotions, many people neglect strong emotions such as anger, sadness and fear. These feelings are what will influence how you handle conflict. Your ability to resolve disputes in conflict will be affected if you fear strong emotions.

Non-Verbal Communication and Conflict Resolution

The most important information to be exchanged in conflict situations is non-verbally. People who become angry rarely express the true feelings of their hearts through the words they use. Listening to both what is being said and what is being felt is key to connecting with your emotions. This type of listening can help you to be more informed, stronger, and easier for others to hear.

You should pay attention to non-verbal communication when you're in conflict. This will help you understand what they really mean and allow you to respond in a way that builds trust and gets to the root cause of the problem. People who are emotionally intelligent have a greater chance of resolving conflict because they can place themselves in the shoes and experiences of the other side.

Chapter Thirteen

Mastering Your Interpersonal Skills for Higher Emotional Intelligence

Anyone who wants to grow their personal and professional skills is sure to benefit from them. This is what separates the great from the average person. People with excellent interpersonal skills are considered more emotionally intelligent and friendlier. These soft skills can be used to improve your communication with others. These are the top interpersonal skills you should have to increase your emotional intelligence.

Verbal communication

The most common form of self-expression is verbal communication. We respond to the world around us, and then communicate our emotions using the words we use. You must ensure that your verbal communication is clear if you want people to understand you. Speaking more thoughtfully is one of the best ways to develop clarity. People will respect your thoughtfulness and be more patient with you.

Communication that is not verbal

It is often overlooked and underrated. Because it reinforces what your verbally expresses, non-verbal communication can have a huge impact on your emotional intelligence. You can communicate emotion or respond to a conversation with out saying a word. Your body language speaks volumes about how you feel. Your body language, posture, voice and gestures can reveal how you feel about the people around.

Listening

Listening is an essential personal skill that allows you to understand and respond to conversations. If your listening skills are inadequate, messages can easily be misunderstood and communication can break down. This can lead to frustration for both parties. It is important to make an effort to improve your listening skills. This will help you increase productivity, customer satisfaction, and share relevant information.

Questioning

Today, asking questions has been deemed a lost art. However, it is a valuable technique that can help to improve listening skills. Contrary to popular belief, asking questions is not just a way to get information but a great way to start conversations.

Asking questions demonstrates your interest

In the topic being discussed. Smart questions show that you are able to ask intelligent questions to find the answers you seek.

Problem Solving

Life is just a series of problems that need to be solved. It doesn't matter how fast you solve the problem. There is no guarantee that your plan will work in problem-solving. Problem-solving is about being able identify the problem and then to analyze the challenges to fully understand them. Then, you need to come up with a strategy to solve the problem.

Social Awareness

Emotional intelligence is about being able to understand the feelings and needs of others. Social awareness allows us to embrace and appreciate others' success. You can also identify opportunities. It is an indication that you have higher emotional intelligence and can respond to social situations in a timely manner.

Chapter Fourteen

Conclusion

Many people mistakenly confuse intelligence quotient and emotional intelligence. You will have greater control over your life if you learn to manage your emotions. This will allow you to unlock new opportunities that you might not have had otherwise. Everyone should strive to attain high emotional intelligence. You shouldn't let this discourage you. Instead, you should keep pressing on to achieve your emotional goals.

Emotional intelligence is a way to learn and train how to better connect with others. It is becoming more important than ever to learn how listen and interpret information from others, especially in this globalized world. This will allow you to learn.

How to communicate with others and structure your responses. Higher emotional intelligence will lead to greater success in your professional and personal lives.

Printed in Great Britain
by Amazon